I0842196

IS-453: Introduction To Homeland Security Planning

By

Fema

10/31/2013

Lesson 1: Introduction to Planning

Course Overview

This course is meant to be an introduction to and an overview of homeland security planning. The primary goal of this course is to familiarize all DHS employees with basic planning knowledge and to encourage them to learn more about the planning process. A secondary goal of this course is to introduce basic analytical and planning skills.

Upon completion of this course, you should be able to:

- Describe homeland security planning
- Describe characteristics of effective planning
- Recognize how the planning process and tools lead to increased homeland security preparedness
- Describe the planning considerations associated with the National Preparedness Mission Areas: Prevention, Protection, Mitigation, Response, and Recovery
- Apply knowledge of homeland security preparedness to a given scenario

Screen Features

- Click the **Exit** button to close this window and access the menu listing all the lessons of this course. You can select any of the lessons from this menu by simply clicking on the lesson title.
- Click the **Glossary** button to look up key definitions and acronyms.
- Click the **Help** button to review guidance and troubleshooting advice regarding navigating through the course.
- Track your progress by looking at the Progress bar at the top right of each screen. To see a numeric display, roll your mouse over the Progress bar area.
- Follow the bold green instructions that appear on each screen in order to proceed to the next screen or complete a Knowledge Review or Activity.

Click the **Back** or **Next** button at the top and bottom of screens to move backward or forward in the lesson. Note: If the **Next** button is dimmed, you must complete an activity before you can proceed in the lesson.

Navigating Using Your Keyboard

Below are instructions for navigating through the course using your keyboard:

- Use the Tab key to move forward through each screen's navigation buttons and hyperlinks, or Shift + Tab to move backwards.
- Press Enter to select a navigation button or hyperlink.

- Use the arrow keys to select answers for multiple-choice review questions or self-assessment checklists. Then tab to the **Submit** button and press **Enter** to complete a Knowledge Review or Self-Assessment.
- Warning: Repeatedly pressing **Tab** beyond the number of selections on the screen may cause the keyboard to lock up. Use Ctrl + Tab to de-select an element or reset to the beginning of a screen's navigation links (most often needed for screens with animations or media).
- Users of JAWS assistive technology can press the Ctrl key to quiet the screen reader while the course audio plays.

Course Features: Receiving Credit

To receive credit for the course you must complete the final exam with a minimum score of 75%. You can access the exam from the course description page or from the last screen of Lesson 5.

If you exit from the course, you will need to start the lesson from which you exited over again.

Course Features: Knowledge Review and Scenarios

Knowledge Review screens provide activities for review of the lesson materials. Instructions appear at the top of the screen explaining how to complete the activity. After the activity has been completed, a pop-up window will appear with feedback.

There are several scenarios in the course. Lesson 5 consists solely of a scenario-based Knowledge Review planning activity that allows you to apply the content and information from the first four lessons to a scenario learning activity. It will be tailored to the mission area in which your work primarily falls. Follow the screen instructions to complete the activity.

Course Features: Links, Resources, and Job Aids

Within the course, you will see blue underlined text which indicates a selectable link. This link will take you either to a website that can provide you with additional information or to a document in the resources for the course.

The resources for additional information and reference are in portable document format (.PDF) and can be opened directly from the resources page. Once the PDF is opened, you can review it, save it to your computer, or print it for future reference.

Job Aids consisting of tips, checklists, and other information that should be printed for future reference are indicated by a selectable Job Aid icon. When this is selected, a PDF document will be displayed which you can print or save to your computer.

Course Introduction

Emergencies and disasters, both natural and man-made, can happen at any time, often without warning. DHS strives to provide its workforce and the nation with tools and training to prevent, protect from, mitigate, respond to, and recover from potential emergencies and disasters.

Homeland security planning is essential to help ensure that we are prepared. This course is part of the Employee Preparedness Initiative (EPI) designed to support and advance a culture of "One DHS" and to mature and strengthen the homeland security enterprise by fostering unity of effort. It is important to realize that preparedness is a shared responsibility. As a DHS employee, regardless of whether or not your job duties include direct planning responsibilities, it is vital that you have an understanding of planning and your role in homeland security planning.

You should know how to plan effectively and how to use planning processes and tools. Lastly, you should know the planning considerations associated with preparedness and how they may affect your job functions.

Think of it like this: The likelihood that you and your family will survive a house fire depends as much on your having a working smoke detector and pre-planned escape routes as it does on having a well-trained fire department in your area. With the proper knowledge and planning, you can help meet the DHS goals and also ensure that you, your fellow employees, and your family are prepared in the event of an emergency or disaster.

Lesson Overview

As a DHS employee, you should do some form of planning—both in your professional and in your personal life. Regardless of your job title, job description, or role, planning should be a part of what you do.

This lesson is an introduction and overview of planning, homeland security planning, and the role planning plays in preparedness.

Upon completion of this lesson, you should be able to:

- Define planning
- State the purpose of planning
- State the benefits of planning
- Describe homeland security planning
- Describe the role of planning in preparedness

What Is Planning?

<u>Presidential Policy Directive 8: National Preparedness (PPD-8)</u> describes the nation's approach to preparing for threats and hazards. It identifies key components to improve national preparedness for these threats and hazards. Planning is not only one of these key components, it is also instrumental in carrying out the other key components.

Planning is a methodical way to think through the entire life cycle of an organizational problem or a potential crisis. Planning provides a systematic process to engage the whole community in:

- Determining required capabilities
- Establishing a framework for roles and responsibilities
- Envisioning desired outcomes
- Selecting ways to achieve those desired outcomes

Planning at DHS

Planning is a tool commonly used throughout DHS.

DHS uses planning as a tool in:

- Strategic thinking
- Problem solving
- Decision making

DHS uses planning as a tool in:

- Leading intra-agency and interagency teams
- Working with intra-agency and interagency teams
- Intra-Agency and interagency Operations

DHS uses planning as a tool in managing and conducting:

- Risk Management
- Incident Management
- Crisis Management

DHS uses planning as a tool in:

- Sharing intelligence and information
- Applying experience
- Applying new ideas

Planning Perspectives

As a DHS employee, regardless of whether or not your job is directly related to planning, you use planning in some form. Review the experiences of each of the following DHS employees to learn about how each uses planning in completing his or her job tasks.

Connie, Senior Policy Analyst
National Protection and Programs Directorate

My main job activity is to develop cyber security policy for the Federal civilian departments and agencies. I develop plans to assess departments and agencies for compliance and to assess Government cyber security posture. The majority of this work is done on an interagency basis. The planning processes and best practices are part of what I do every day.

James, Manager
Transportation Security Administration (TSA)-Intermodal Security Support Division

At TSA, we use planning to develop national security strategies and plans in accordance with Federal requirements. We also use planning to develop national-level operational plans and field-level tactical plans to meet requirements for the incidents within the TSA's mission scope.

Robert, Chief
U.S. Coast Guard (USCG)-Office of Counterterrorism and Defense Operations

At USCG, planning is used in all aspects of my every-day job duties—from informal internal issues that require a disciplined approach to develop viable options (Courses of Action) to formal interagency planning efforts. Planning is also used in annual cycles of reviewing the Department of Defense contingency plans.

Benefits of Planning

Planning is considered one of the key success factors in protecting people and property in crises.

Planning is essential and beneficial because it:

- Positions you to be ready to act
  - Shortens time required to gain control of an incident
  - Reduces time between decision and action during operations
- Provides understanding of potentially complex situations
- Allows you to devise a workable solution to unforeseen and/or novel situations
- Provides conditions for rapid and effective exchange of information about a situation, its analysis, and alternative responses

- Helps Federal, State, Local, Tribal, and Territorial government to be more interoperable
- Helps planners be more agile in adapting to the dynamic environment and stakeholder requirements
- Ensures that organizational structures, processes, and procedures support the intended strategic direction effectively
- Enables continuity of services we depend on, such as:
    - Receiving salary
        - Security and safe

CPG 101 Benefits of Planning

The <u>Comprehensive Preparedness Guide (CPG) 101</u> document provides guidance on developing emergency operations plans, and states that the benefits of planning are as follows:

- It brings unity of purpose through coordination and integration of plans across all levels of government , non-governmental organizations (NGOs), the private sector, individuals, and families
- It provides logical and analytical problem-solving processes
- It addresses complexity and uncertainty inherent in potential hazards and threats

Homeland Security Planning

PPD-8, the Presidential Policy Directive that deals with National Preparedness, required the development of a national preparedness system and a national preparedness goal. *The National Preparedness Goal* was issued in September 2011.

The National Preparedness Goal defines planning as "conducting a systematic process engaging the whole community as appropriate in the development of executable strategic, operational, and/or community-based approaches to meet defined objectives."

Mission Areas

The *National Preparedness Goal* identifies core capabilities grouped into Mission Areas that are critical to preparing successfully for threats and hazards to our nation. Below is a brief introduction to the Mission Areas.

Prevention

Prevention includes those capabilities necessary to avoid, prevent, or stop a threatened or actual act of terrorism. It is focused on ensuring that we are optimally prepared to prevent an imminent terrorist attack within the United States.

Protection

Protection includes capabilities to safeguard the homeland against acts of terrorism and man-made or natural disasters. It is focused on actions to protect our citizens, residents, visitors, and critical assets, systems, and networks against the greatest risk to our nation in a manner that allows our interests, aspirations, and way of life to thrive.

Mitigation

Mitigation includes those capabilities necessary to reduce loss of life and property by lessening the impact of disasters. It is focused on the premise that individuals, the private sector, communities, critical infrastructure, and the nation as a whole are made more resilient when the consequences and impacts, the duration, and the financial and human costs to respond to and recover from adverse incidents are all reduced.

Response

Response includes those capabilities necessary to save lives, protect property and the environment, and meet basic human needs after an incident has occurred. It is focused on ensuring that the nation is able to respond effectively to any threat or hazard, including those with cascading effects, with an emphasis on saving and sustaining lives and stabilizing the incident, as well as rapidly meeting basic human needs, restoring basic services and community functionality, establishing a safe and secure environment, and supporting the transition to recovery.

Recovery

Recovery includes those capabilities necessary to assist communities affected by an incident to recover effectively. It is focused on a timely restoration, strengthening, and revitalization of the infrastructure; housing; a sustainable economy; and the health, social, cultural, historic, and environmental fabric of communities affected by a catastrophic event.

Planning and Homeland Security Preparedness

Planning is one of the key components of homeland security preparedness. There are three levels of planning.

Tactical Planning

Tactical planning is the detailed identification and development of goals, priorities, objectives, and actions tailored to specific situations and fact patterns at an operational level. It is meant to support and achieve the objectives of the operational plan.

Operational Planning

Operational planning is the process by which specific personnel, resource, and asset allocations are made to execute the objectives of the strategic plan. An operational plan contains a full description of the concept of operations with supporting annexes.

Strategic Planning

Strategic planning is the process by which:

- Requirements are generated
- Long-range goals, priorities, and objectives are established
- Responsibilities are agreed upon

This is where performance and effectiveness measures are developed and applied in order to execute upper Government policy.

Planning and Personal Preparedness

As we discussed earlier, in order to protect you and your loved ones from potential emergency or disaster, you must be prepared—and in order to be prepared, you must plan!

In an emergency or disaster, it is important to remember that you and your family may not be together, so make sure to plan:

- How each of you will get to a safe place
- How you will contact one another
- How and where you will meet up
- What you will do in different situations

Ready.gov is a great resource for you and your family as you are making your Family Emergency Plans. The website provides templates for developing your plan, as well as instructions for putting together a disaster supplies kit.

Lesson Summary

This lesson provided an introduction to planning, homeland security preparedness, and the role of planning in preparedness. You should now be able to:

- Define planning
- State the purpose of planning
- State the benefits of planning
- Describe homeland security planning

- Describe the role of planning in preparedness

Some key points from this lesson include:

- As a DHS employee, you should do some form of planning—both in your professional and in your personal life.
- Planning is a tool commonly used by DHS in a variety of situations.
- Planning is considered one of the key success factors in protecting people and property.
- Planning brings unity of purpose through coordination and integration across all levels of government, NGOs, private sectors, individuals, and families.

In Lesson 2, we will discuss the basic characteristics of effective planning.

Lesson 2: Planning Basics

Lesson Overview

This lesson will provide you with an overview of the characteristics of effective planning and tips, tools, and techniques that will help to enhance your planning efforts. In Lesson 3: Planning Process and Tools, we will have a more in-depth discussion of the specific tasks and activities in a planning process.

Upon completion of this lesson, you should be able to:

- List the benefits of using a planning development process
- Describe the benefits of using a team in planning
- Explain critical and creative thinking as applied to the planning process
- Identify additional tips, tools, and techniques to enhance planning

Planning Processes

One of the most important characteristics of successful planning efforts is the use of a defined planning process. There are several different planning processes used by Government entities and by the private sector. Some examples of Government/public-sector planning processes include:

- Federal Plan Development Process (FPDP)
- Comprehensive Preparedness Guide (CPG) 101
- National Incident Management System (NIMS) Planning P
- Hazard Mitigation Planning Process

An example of a private-sector planning process is the Six Sigma Define, Measure, Analyze, Improve, Control (DMAIC) method.

Regardless of the planning process you use, the fundamental common activities/tasks for these planning processes are to:

- Determine the problem you are trying to solve
- Develop an analytical approach to determine as much about the problem as possible
- Develop alternative options on how to solve the problem
- Complete the writing of the plan, involving as much of the community of interest as possible
- Conduct periodic testing and reviews of plan

Benefits of Using Planning Processes

Regardless of which specific planning process you use, the two most important things to keep in mind are that you are using a well-defined planning process and that a well-defined process results in a more effective, innovative, affordable, and flexible solution.

Planning processes provide a logical and analytical problem-solving method. Planning processes help to address the complexity and uncertainty of many planning efforts. They can help reduce confusion in the early stages of planning and facilitate agreement on assumptions.

Following a planning process helps to meet the senior leader's goals and objectives.

Planning processes help to ensure that important inputs are considered.

Benefits of Planning in Teams

Experience has shown that to ensure a successful planning effort, the planning should be done as a team.

More Inclusive of Stakeholders

Planning should be a community-based effort, representing the whole population and its needs. Planning in a team environment allows participation from stakeholders and ensures that the needs of each stakeholder group are addressed.

More Varied Insight

Each person on the planning team brings different experiences, opinions, and expertise to the planning effort. Planning in a team helps to bring creativity and innovation to the plan. Planning in a team encourages creativity and innovation in the plan.

Consensus Building

Planning in teams allows for members of the team to understand and accept their roles. In addition, it helps members of the team understand and accept the roles of other planning team members.

Greater Access to Resources

Planning in teams helps to leverage the knowledge and expertise of a diverse group of planning team members. It means that available resources can be pooled. For example, your agency may not have a records management expert, but another agency or department may have this resource available to participate on the planning team.

Forming Cooperative Relationships

Experience has shown that one of the greatest benefits of planning teams is that they build and expand relationships that are vital when the plan is put into action (response to an incident occurrence, implementation of a protection or prevention plan, conducting recovery activities). Incidents often require cross-functional and multijurisdictional response, and professional relationships that are developed during the planning process should translate into better cooperation and coordination.

Sense of Ownership

The plan is more likely to be followed if the agencies, departments, and/or organizations feel as if they have contributed to it.

Critical and Creative Thinking

Another characteristic that is fundamental to a successful planning effort is the use of both critical and creative thinking in the planning process.

Critical Thinking

Critical thinking can be defined as the active, persistent, and careful consideration of any belief or supposed form of knowledge in the light of the grounds that support it and the further conclusions to which it tends.

—Alex Fisher, Critical Thinking: An Introduction.

Cambridge University Press, 2001.

Critical thinking is that mode of thinking in which the thinker improves the quality of his or her thinking by skillfully taking charge of the structures inherent in thinking and imposing intellectual standards upon them.

-Paul and Elder, 2001.

Foundation for Critical Thinking.

Critical thinking can be described as the intellectually disciplined process of actively and skillfully conceptualizing, applying, analyzing, synthesizing, and/or evaluating information gathered from, or generated by, observation, experience, reflection, reasoning, or communication. It is a guide to belief and reasonable, reflective thinking that is focused on deciding what to do or believe.

Creative Thinking

Creative thinking can be defined as the creation or generation of ideas, processes, experiences, or objects. Creative thinking involves creating something new or original and involves the skills of flexibility, brainstorming, imagery, metaphorical thinking, and associative thinking. The aim of creative thinking is to stimulate curiosity, imagination, and promote divergence.

Creative thinking can happen in every organization—even large bureaucracies! It is necessary for working effectively at DHS and to be successful in the interagency environment.

Critical Thinking and Planning

Critical thinking and creative thinking are equally important to planning. They're interrelated, and learning to do both well will increase your effectiveness in completing job tasks that require planning.

Critical thinking is important in planning because it helps to:

- Raise and define questions and problems and ensure that the questions and problems are clear and precise
- Provide structure and logical assessment in what may sometimes be hectic, high-stress, or uncertain situations
- Gather and assess relevant information
- Come to well-reasoned conclusions and solutions, testing them against relevant criteria and standards
- Recognize and assess assumptions, implications, and practical consequences
- Communicate effectively with others to figure out solutions to complex problems

Critical Thinking Process

There are many different critical thinking processes, but they have steps in common.

Step 1: Identify the problem

In the first step of critical thinking, you should identify the problem/incident you are planning for by:

- Assembling specific known facts
- Listing what you think you know
- Identifying what is not known

Step 2: Consider all information without bias

Do not rush to a hypothesis or jump to a conclusion about the problem or incident. When you can look at all of the data without bias, you can avoid jumping to conclusions, look systematically at the issue you are planning for, and come up with every possible alternative.

Step 3: Recognize stated and unstated assumptions

When you settle on one idea or assumption, you may ignore evidence pointing to other possibilities. The best planners let the facts, requirements, and constraints guide them, rather than trying to fit the situation into what they have already concluded.

Step 4: Develop pertinent questions

Critical questions are those that need to be answered to solve the problem or understand the incident. Questions may be different depending on what we think the problem is, so make sure you have the problem clearly identified and agreed upon. These questions lead to analytic recommendations.

Critical Thinking and the Elements of Thought

Drs. Paul and Elder of The Foundation for Critical Thinking developed the "Elements of Thought," which differentiates all thinking into eight related steps (Paul and Elder, 2008). These elements of thought align with the standard process for critical thinking. Review the following Elements of Thought.

All reasoning has a purpose

- State your purpose clearly.
- Distinguish your purpose from related purposes.
- Check periodically to be sure you are still on target.
- Choose significant and realistic purposes.

All reasoning is an attempt to figure something out, to settle some question, to solve some problem

- State he question at issue clearly and precisely.
- Express the question in several ways to clarify its meaning and scope.
- Break the question into sub-questions.
- Distinguish questions that have definitive answers from those that are a matter of opinion and from those that require consideration of multiple viewpoints.

All reasoning is based on data, information and evidence

- Restrict your claims to those supported by the data you have.
- Search for information that opposes your position as well as information that supports it.
- Make sure that all information used is clear, accurate, and relevant to the question at issue.

- Make sure you have gathered sufficient information.

All reasoning contains inferences or interpretations by which we draw conclusions and give meaning to data

- Infer only what the evidence implies.
- Check inferences for their consistency with each other.
- Identify assumptions that lead to inferences.

All reasoning is expressed through, and shaped by, concepts and ideas

- Identify key concepts and explain them clearly.
- Consider alternative concepts or alternative definitions of concepts.
- Make sure you are using concepts with care and precision.

All reasoning is based on assumptions

- Clearly identify your assumptions and determine whether they are justifiable.
- Consider how your assumptions are shaping your point of view.

All reasoning leads somewhere or has implications andconsequences

- Trace the implications and consequences that follow from your reasoning.
- Search for negative as well as positive implications.
- Consider all possible consequences.

All reasoning is done from some point of view

- Identify your point of view.
- Seek other points of view and identify their strengths as well as weaknesses.
- Strive to be fair-minded in evaluating all points of view.

Creative Thinking and Planning

Creative thinking is important in planning because it helps to:

- Develop imaginative or innovative, but accurate and effective, ways to fulfill a requirement
- Generate ideas at the start of the planning effort (brainstorming)
- Open up planning team members to each other's perspectives
- Increase flexibility and ability to deal with the changing and unpredictable nature of many incidents

Creative Thinking Process

Creative thinking, just like critical thinking, follows a process

Challenge the Rules

Our thinking is often governed by rules that limit us to the patterns we have already formed in our minds. The rules are sometimes so engrained that we don't even realize we have them, so we don't realize that we are limiting our creativity.

This strategy identifies those rules and challenges them. By developing challenges for the rules, we put a "block" in the main track of our thought processes, which allows us to take a step back and see alternatives we might otherwise have ignored.

Shift Focus

This strategy is a way to get your mind off the main track and onto a "side track." By simply changing the focus of your attention, you force yourself to see new perspectives.

Connect Different Ideas

This strategy involves bringing previously unrelated information and ideas together in new and meaningful ways. In this case, the goal is to get onto the "side track" from a completely different place. Rather than starting from the main track of thought and trying to change your perspective, you "jump" onto a side path before the pattern of the main track is too engrained.

Additional Tips, Tools, and Techniques

Below are additional tips, tools, and techniques related to the characteristics for a successful planning effort. You can choose to review these now, or you can print them and review them at your leisure.

The Tips for Forming Collaborative Teams provides some considerations and guidelines for forming your planning team. In addition, it gives tips to ensure the success of the team.
(See Resources page for this document)

The Elements of Thought Checklist is a checklist for critical thinking that can be used as you are working your way through the planning process.
(See Resources page for this document)

The Planning Questions Based on Elements of Thought Job Aid contains specific planning-related questions that can be used in your planning effort.
(See Resources page for this document)

The <u>Tips for Incorporating Creative Thinking Job Aid</u> contains tips and information about how to incorporate creative thinking into your planning effort.
(See Resources page for this document)

Lesson Summary

This lesson provided you with an overview of the characteristics of effective planning and tips, tools, and techniques that will help to enhance your planning efforts. You should now be able to:

- List the benefits of using a planning development process
- Describe the benefits of using a team in planning
- Explain critical and creative thinking as applied to the planning process
- Identify additional tips, tools, and techniques to enhance planning

Some key points from this lesson include:

- Using a defined planning process is critical in the success of the planning effort.
- Planning in teams has many benefits and is critical to the success of the planning effort, as well as affecting the outcome of any Prevention, Protection, Mitigation, Response, and Recovery activities.
- Critical and creative thinking allows you to conduct planning in a way that improves problem solving, and guides planners to:
  - Think before doing
  - Use forward thinking to influence events
  - Intervene in the present to ensure positive results in the future

In Lesson 3, we will have a more in-depth discussion of the specific steps in a planning process, and you will have the chance to apply to a scenario some of the planning basics—including critical and creative thinking—discussed in this lesson.

Lesson 3: Planning Process and Tools

Lesson Overview

This lesson will provide you with a more in-depth look at the planning process steps, as well as providing an opportunity for you to apply critical and creative thinking to a planning-related activity

Upon completion of this lesson, you should be able to:

- Identify common planning process steps
- Given a homeland security planning situation, use critical thinking
- Given a homeland security planning situation, use creative thinking

Planning Processes

As we discussed in Lesson 2, there are several planning processes that are in use today. The various processes have common planning steps.

Regardless of which planning process you use, the activities you will be performing will be very similar. For the purposes of this course, we will discuss the common process identified in National Incident Management System (NIMS), Federal Plan Development Process (FPDP), Comprehensive Planning Guide (CPG) 101, and the FEMA Regional Planning Guide.

Form a Collaborative Team

Homeland security planning is a team effort requiring coordination between agencies and organizations at different levels of government. Additionally, different types of incidents require different types of expertise and responses. The planning effort will benefit from the active participation of stakeholders.

One major activity in Form a Collaborative Team is determining team membership. The members of the team are determined by the objectives of the planning effort. You want to ensure that you are including all members of the community of interest.

Successful Collaboration

Successful team collaboration requires a:

- Commitment to participate in shared decision making
- Willingness to share information, resources, and tasks
- Professional respect for individual team members, their ideas, and their opinions

Obstacles to successful collaborative teams include differences between agencies and organizations in:

- Terminology
- Experience
- Mission
- Culture

You know your team is on track when it starts to display the following characteristics:

- A common goal and purpose
- A leader who provides direction and guidance
- Open communication
- Constructive conflict resolution
- Mutual trust and respect

Understand the Situation

To understand the situation fully, planners need to conduct research on the planning topic, and determine what leadership desires as a successful outcome or end state. The two main activities in Understand the Situation are to:

- Determine facts and assumptions
- Perform risk assessment
    - Identify the hazards and threats
    - Assess risk

Understand the Situation—Facts and Assumptions

Facts and assumptions are used to help define the planning problem.

Facts

Definition: verified pieces of information, such as laws, regulations, terrain maps, population statistics, resource inventories, and prior occurrences. Initial resource availability and capabilities are key facts that should be included.

Examples:

- Type of chemical spilled or released and its characteristics
- Hardening put in place in order to prevent an explosive from breaching a protective wall to a facility
- Historically, the number of individuals who did not evacuate from an area expected to be hit by a natural disaster

- Number of law enforcement personnel available for an operation from different sources
- Number of hospital beds available in an area

Assumptions

Definition: consists of information accepted by planners as being true in the absence of facts in order to provide a framework or establish expected conditions of an operational environment so that planning can proceed. Assumptions are used as facts only if they are considered **valid** (or likely to be true) and are **necessary** for solving the problem.

Examples:

- Storm surge of 25 feet will top local sea wall by 5 feet
- Cyber attack will originate from outside the U.S.
- Cascading effects of earthquake damage will include fires such as those from broken natural gas lines
- Chemical release will be in U.S. Coast Guard (USCG) area of responsibility
- Criminal aliens will be involved in the terrorist attack
- Temporary housing will be needed as part of the recovery effort

Understand the Situation—Threat Analysis

Identifying, researching, and analyzing information about potential threats and hazards is a key activity in Understand the Situation. Threat analysis determines:

- What can occur
- How it will occur
- How often it is likely to occur
- The consequences that can occur
- How it will affect the communities in which it occurs
- How vulnerable we are to the threat

Example:

What can occur?

Human-Caused: Drugs, maritime disasters, smuggling, oil spills

Natural Disasters: Hurricane, wildfire

How will it occur?

Human-Caused: Crimes, accidents, terrorist-related

Natural Disasters: Weather-related

How often is it likely to occur?

Human-Caused: Based on statistical data

Natural Disasters: Seasonally

What consequences can occur?

Human-Caused: Economic loss, degradation in the quality of life, decrease of property value, environmental damage

Natural Disasters: Loss of life, flooding, power outages, damage to property, economic damage

What actions would the community need to take to deal with the threat/hazard?

Human-Caused: Law enforcement, first responder, community activists, hazardous materials response teams, public relations

Natural Disasters: Evacuation, sheltering, health care, mental health care

How vulnerable are we to the threat?

Human-Caused: Based on the level of preparedness, effectiveness of prevention and protection activities

Natural Disasters: Based on the level of preparedness (i.e. do we have a sea wall built to prevent flooding?)

Determine Goals and Objectives

Goals and objectives must be developed carefully to ensure that they support accomplishing the planning mission and operational priorities. They should also clearly indicate the desired end state—what is the end product of the planning effort. This helps to ensure unity of effort and consistency of purpose among the multiple departments, agencies, and organizations involved in the planning effort.

Goals are broad, general statements that indicate the intended solution to problems identified in Understand the Situation.

Objectives are more specific and are actions carried out during the execution of the plan.

Determine Goals and Objectives—Mission Statement

Determining goals and objectives lead to developing a mission statement for your plan. The mission statement includes:

- Who will do the action?
- What must occur?
- When should the action occur?
- Where should the action occur?
- Why is the action required?

The mission statement does not include **how** the action should occur. The **how** is included in developing courses of action (COA).

After developing the mission statement, a best practice is to ensure that senior leadership has reviewed and endorses the statement and that the goals and objectives are aligned with the desired end state.

Sample Recovery Mission Statement

After a tornado, the recovery community of Washington County will conduct recovery planning and operations within the entire county in order to restore community infrastructure, housing, services, and economic activity.

- **Who:** Recovery community of Washington County
- **What:** Conduct recovery planning and operations
- **When:** After a tornado
- **Where:** Within the entire county
- **Why:** Restore community infrastructure, housing, services, and economic activity

Develop, Compare, and Select Courses of Action

In order to achieve the goals and objectives defined previously, we must generate, compare, and select possible courses of action (COAs) or solutions. The planning team, in discussion with leadership, will need to determine how many solutions or alternatives to consider, but it is good practice to consider ,*at least* two options.

Develop COAs

Identify COAs, using brainstorming and other creative thinking methods to generate various solutions to achieve the mission effectively.

Remember: In order for brainstorming to be effective, it must be done in a collaborative and open environment

Analyze COAs, using critical thinking methods, to identify and depict operational tasks. This involves identifying and describing all of the steps/tasks required to perform the course of action such as:

- What is the task (description)?
- Who would perform the task?
- When will the task take place?
- What resources are needed to perform the tasks?
- In what sequence are the tasks performed?

Compare COAs

Based upon criteria established by the planning team, COAs are evaluated in order to determine their respective strengths and weaknesses.

Select a COA

The COA that is best able to meet the objectives is selected as the concept of operations for the plan.

Example COA

This is an example of developing and comparing COAs, and then selecting one.

The mission statement previously provided: *After a tornado, the recovery community of Washington County will conduct recovery planning and operations within the entire county in order to restore community infrastructure, housing, services, and economic activity.*

COA 1: Develop a community task force that focuses on re-establishing public utilities throughout the community and creates a sub-task force for housing and park development. Funding will be provided through Federal and State grants.

Re-establishing public utilities as a first step will encourage the population to return to the damaged areas and begin personal and commercial/business restoration efforts.

COA 2: Establish the Mayor's Community Recovery Office for public services, and to enable individuals to obtain grants for restoring their damaged property.

Funding will be provided through a community tax and may be supported through limited Federal and State grants.

Offering personal reconstruction grants will encourage the population to return to the damaged area and begin restoration.

After the two COAs are compared, COA 1 is considered the best choice to achieve the mission statement, based on the criteria of funding availability, recovery timeframe, and ease of implementation.

Develop, Compare, and Select Courses of Action— Review Resources

Once a course of action is selected, the planning team should review the previously identified resources to determine whether they are sufficient to carry out the COA. The outcome of your resource review can be:

- Resources are sufficient
  - Move forward with plan development
- Additional resources are required
  - Acquire additional resources
  - Modify COA to match resource availability
- Resources cannot be realistically or readily obtained for the selected COA
  - Change to a different COA for which resources are adequate and available
  - Develop a new COA that matches the resources

Develop the Plan

This is a culmination of the work done previously. It turns the course of action into an executable plan. A best practice is to write the plan initially as a draft. The planning team should also solicit comments from the community of interest, adjudicate them, and include the appropriate comments in the final version.

The planning team reviews the plan to ensure that it is effective and efficient, and that it complies with any applicable regulatory requirements.

Once validated and reviewed, the plan should be presented to the appropriate senior leaders for official approval. After approval, the planning team arranges to distribute the plan to the community of interest.

Implement, Evaluate, and Revise the Plan

After the plan is approved and disseminated, personnel will need to be trained so they have the knowledge, skills, and abilities needed to perform the tasks identified in the plan. Personnel should also be trained on the organization-specific procedures necessary to support the plan tasks.

Developing and implementing multi-organizational training events and exercises will help to evaluate the effectiveness of the plan and to determine whether the goals, objectives, decisions, and actions outlined in the plan lead to success.

Remember that planning is a cyclical process. After the training, exercising, and implementation of the plan, the plan should be updated and revised incorporating any lessons learned. The planning team should establish a process for reviewing and revising the plan. Some events that should trigger the review or revision of the plan include:

- Major incident
- Change in policy or other operational requirement
- Major exercise
- Change in hazard or threat profile

Lesson Summary

This lesson provided you with an in-depth look at the stages of the planning process, as well as providing an opportunity for you to apply critical and creative thinking to a planning-related activity. You should now be able to:

- Identify common planning processes
- Given a homeland security planning situation, use critical thinking
- Given a homeland security planning situation, use creative thinking

Some key points from this lesson include:

- Regardless of the specific planning process you use, the tasks you perform are basically the same.
- Critical thinking can ensure well-thought-out plans.
- Creative thinking can help to create innovative and flexible plans.

In Lesson 4, we will discuss planning considerations related to the Preparedness Mission Areas.

Lesson 4: Preparedness Planning Considerations by Mission Areas

Lesson Overview

In this lesson we will discuss each of the mission areas, and the planning requirements, activities, and specific mission-area-related considerations associated with each.

Upon completion of this lesson, you should be able to:

- Identify planning considerations for Prevention
- Identify planning considerations for Protection
- Identify planning considerations for Mitigation
- Identify planning considerations for Response
- Identify planning considerations for Recovery

Planning Core Capability

The *National Preparedness Goal* identified core capabilities for each of the homeland security mission areas—Prevention, Protection, Mitigation, Response, and Recovery (P/P/M/R/R). The core capabilities are the critical elements necessary for ensuring the nation's safety and achieving the *National Preparedness Goal*. Planning is one of only three core capabilities common to all of the mission areas.

Planning for each of the mission areas provides a systematic process that engages the whole community as appropriate in the development of executable strategic, operational, and/or tactical approaches to meet defined objectives.

For the remainder of the lesson, we will discuss:

- The definition of each mission area
- The description, requirements, and activities related to planning for each mission area
- The planning considerations for each mission area
- The additional core capabilities for each mission area

Prevention Mission Area

Definition of Mission Area:

Prevention includes those capabilities necessary to avoid, prevent, or stop a threatened or actual act of terrorism. Unlike the other mission areas, which are all-hazards, PPD-8 specifically designates prevention-related activities for terrorist threats.

Planning Core Capability Target:

1. Identify critical objectives based on the planning requirement, provide a complete and integrated picture of the sequence and scope of the tasks to achieve the objectives, and ensure that the objectives are implementable within the timeframe contemplated in the plan using available resources for prevention-related plans.
2. Develop and execute appropriate courses of action in coordination with Federal, State, Local, and private-sector entities in order to prevent a terrorist attack within the United States.

Planning Considerations:

1. Prevention and Protection actions, including planning, occur prior to, during, and after an incident.
2. Terrorist threats are dynamic and complex.
3. It is not the sole responsibility of a single entity or community to combat terrorism.
4. Following an incident, Prevention actions would include a collaborative investigative process that includes the systematic collection and analysis of information suspected of being, contributing to, or having caused, a terrorist threat or incident.

Other Core Capabilities:

In addition to planning, the other core capabilities of the prevention mission area are:

- Public Information and Warning
- Operational Coordination
- Forensics and Attribution
- Intelligence and Information Sharing
- Interdiction and Disruption
- Screening, Search, and Detection

For additional information on each of these core capabilities, review the *National Preparedness Goal* available on the resources page.

Protection Mission Area

Definition of Mission Area:

Protection includes capabilities to safeguard the homeland against acts of terrorism and man-made or natural disasters. It is focused on action to protect the citizens, residents, visitors, and critical assets, systems, and networks against the greatest risk to our Nation in a manner that allows our interests, aspirations, and way of life to thrive.

Planning Core Capability Target:

1. Develop protection plans that identify critical objectives based on planning requirements, provide a complete and integrated picture of the sequence and scope of the tasks to achieve the planning objectives, and implement planning requirements within the timeframe contemplated in the plan using available resources for protection-related plans.
2. Implement, exercise, and maintain plans to ensure continuity of operations (COOP).

Planning Considerations:

1. The Protection core capabilities are achieved through specific mission activities. In planning for the Protection Mission Area, it is important to keep in mind these mission activities, which include, but are not limited to:
   - Critical infrastructure protection
   - Cybersecurity
   - Border security
   - Immigration security
   - Protection of key leadership and events
   - Maritime security
   - Transportation security
   - Defense of agriculture and food
   - Defense against weapons of mass destruction (WMD)
   - Health security
2. Protection is the ability to safeguard the homeland against acts of terrorism as well as human-caused or natural disasters.
3. When writing protection plans, take into account COOP.
4. Prevention and Protection actions, including planning, occur prior to, during, and after an incident.

Other Core Capabilities:

In addition to planning, the other core capabilities of the protection mission area are:

- Public Information and Warning
- Operational Coordination
- Access Control and Identity Verification
- Cybersecurity
- Intelligence and Information Sharing
- Interdiction and Disruption
- Physical Protective Measures
- Risk Management for Protection Programs and Activities
- Screening, Search, and Detection
- Supply Chain Integrity and Security

For additional information on each of these core capabilities, review the *National Preparedness Goal* available on the resources page.

Mitigation Mission Area

Definition of Mission Area:

Mitigation includes those capabilities necessary to reduce loss of life and property by lessening the impact of disasters. Due to the impacts of disasters and catastrophic incidents on the Nation, Mitigation is the most critical element to reduce or eliminate the long-term risks to life, property, and well-being.

Planning Core Capability Target:

1. Develop approved hazard mitigation plans that address all relevant threats/hazards in accordance with the results of risk assessments conducted within all states and territories.

Planning Considerations:

1. Assessment of risk and resilience must begin at the local level and serve to inform state, regional, and national planning.
2. Determine structural (i.e. building of levees) or non-structural (i.e. building codes) initiatives that reduce likelihood of identified incidents occurring or reduce vulnerability to those incidents and/or reduce the consequences of the incident.
3. Determine those projects with the highest return on investment in mitigating potential loss.
4. Remember to plan for:
    a. Persons with access and functional needs
    b. Animals and pets
    c. Private-sector and community involvement
    d. Hard-to-reach or otherwise isolated areas and territories

Other Core Capabilities:

In addition to planning, the other core capabilities of the mitigation mission area are:

- Public Information and Warning
- Operational Coordination
- Community Resilience
- Long-Term Vulnerability Reduction
- Risk and Disaster Resilience Assessment
- Threats and Hazard Identification

For additional information on each of these core capabilities, review the *National Preparedness Goal* available on the resources page.

Response Mission Area

Definition of Mission Area:

Response includes those capabilities necessary to save lives, protect property and the environment, and meet basic human needs after an incident has occurred.

Planning Core Capability Target:

1. Develop operational plans at the Federal and Regional level, and in states and territories, that adequately identify critical objectives based on the planning requirement, provide a complete and integrated picture of the sequence and scope of the tasks to achieve the objectives, and ensure that the objectives are implementable within the timeframe contemplated in the plan using available resources.

Planning Considerations:

1. Communities regularly deal with emergencies and disasters that have impacts of lesser magnitude than those considered to be the greatest risk to the Nation.
2. Communities have capacities to deal with the public's needs locally for many lesser incidents.
3. Take into account the needs of State, Local and Tribal communities.
4. Remember to plan for:

   a. Persons with access and functional needs
   b. Animals and pets
   c. Private-sector and community involvement
   d. Hard-to-reach or otherwise isolated areas and territories

5. Catastrophic incidents will require a much broader set of partners to accomplish capability targets.
6. The scope and magnitude of a catastrophic event can involve legal, policy, and regulatory waivers/exemptions/exceptions to achieve capability targets.
7. These waivers/exemptions/exceptions should be identified during pre-incident planning.

Other Core Capabilities:

In addition to planning, the other core capabilities of the response mission area are:

- Public Information and Warning
- Operational Coordination
- Critical Transportation
- Environmental Response/Health and Safety
- Fatality Management Services

- Infrastructure Systems
- Mass Care Services
- Mass Search and Rescue Operations
- On-scene Security and Protection
- Operational Communications
- Public and Private Services and Resources
- Public Health and Medical Services
- Situational Assessment

For additional information on each of these core capabilities, review the *National Preparedness Goal* available on the resources page.

Recovery Mission Area

Definition of Mission Area:

Recovery includes those capabilities necessary to assist communities affected by an incident in development, coordination, and execution of service- and site-restoration plans.

Planning Core Capability Target:

1. Establish tiered, integrated leadership, and inclusive coordinating organizations that operate with a unity of effort and are supported by sufficient assessment and analysis to provide defined structure and decision-making processes for recovery activities.
2. Define the path and timeline for recovery leadership to achieve the jurisdiction's objectives that effectively coordinate and use appropriate Federal, State, and Local assistance, as well as nongovernmental and private-sector resources. This plan is to be implemented within the established timeline.

Planning Considerations:

1. The ability of a community to accelerate the recovery process begins with its effort in pre-disaster preparedness.
2. Remember that after an incident, recovery is more than the restoration of a community's physical structures.
3. Successful recovery requires informed and coordinated leadership throughout the whole community during all phases of the recovery process.
4. Successful recovery takes into account the linkages between recovery of individuals, families, and communities and addresses the full range of physical, programmatic, communications, psychological, and emotional needs of the community.
5. Remember to plan for:
   a. Persons with access and functional needs
   b. Animals and pets

c. Private-sector and community involvement
d. Hard-to-reach or otherwise isolated areas and territories
e. Needs of response and recovery personnel

Other Core Capabilities:

In addition to planning, the other core capabilities of the recovery mission area are:

- Public Information and Warning
- Operational Coordination
- Economic Recovery
- Health and Social Services
- Housing
- Infrastructure Systems
- Natural and Cultural Resources

For additional information on each of these core capabilities, review the *National Preparedness Goal* available on the resources page.

Relationship Among Mission Areas

It is important to realize that while we discussed each of the mission areas separately, there is an interdependent relationship among the mission areas that is required to meet the planning needs.

Some things to keep in mind include:

- Prevention and Protection actions, including planning, occur prior to, during, and after an incident.
- Response and Recovery are specific to the incident.
- Mitigation is ongoing—always occurring.
    - The effort put into Mitigation should reduce the requirements of Prevention, Protection, Response, and Recovery.
- Planning considerations that are common to all of the mission areas include:
    - Not all resources come from one agency (i.e., Interagency agreements, Legislation establishing multiple agency coordination, Memorandums of Agreement, Memorandums of Understanding, Emergency Management Assistance Compact).
    - Consider stakeholders including Federal, State, Local, Tribal, and private sectors.
    - Consider critical infrastructure and key resources (CIKR).
- It is important that you understand the environment for which you are planning. Keep in mind the cultural and special geospatial features of the area.
- You have finite resources, so you will need to set priorities.
    - What you prioritize is specific to each mission area.
- Identify and define critical communications.

Lesson Summary

In this lesson we discussed each of the mission areas, and the planning requirements, activities, and specific mission-area-related considerations associated with each. You should now be able to:

- Identify planning considerations for Prevention
- Identify planning considerations for Protection
- Identify planning considerations for Mitigation
- Identify planning considerations for Response
- Identify planning considerations for Recovery

Some key points from this lesson include:

- The Prevention mission area is specific to terrorism incidents.
- Planning is a critical element that is common to all of the mission areas.
- Mitigation should reduce the requirements for the other mission areas.
- Success of the *National Preparedness Goal* depends on the interdependent relationship among the mission areas.

In Lesson 5, you will have the opportunity to apply what you have learned about planning to a scenario based on the mission area in which your job falls.

Lesson 5: Planning Learning Activity

Lesson Overview

This lesson consists of a scenario activity that integrates the information that you have learned about planning in the other lessons of this course. It provides you with an opportunity to apply those concepts to a planning scenario based on the mission area in which your job falls.

Scenario Introduction and Background

Central City is a small city in the United States with a population of approximately 20,000. It is located near your current location in the U.S. (if you are outside the U.S., it is near your home office within the United States). It may be adjacent to an international border and/or on the coast. Central City's climate and geography are similar to the climate and geography most representative of the area in which your department/agency/office conducts your missions.

It has typical infrastructure for a small city, but also has freight and passenger rail running through it, with a small passenger terminal and two freight stops, one at the warehouse complex and one at the chemical plant. The nearest municipal airport is 35 miles away, and the nearest commercial airport is 100 miles away. Central City's businesses include typical small-city businesses with a few big-box stores, as well as a chemical processing plant on the edge of the city. Central City has a small U.S. Federal installation near the city limits.

Central City has one high school, one junior high school, and several elementary schools, a small hospital, and several nursing homes. Central City has a police force, fire department, and EMS, and a city emergency manager.

NOTE: You can find the 5 Mission Area specific scenarios, questions, and answers in the lesson. They are not included in this document.

Lesson Summary

Congratulations on completing the scenario! You have done well for the citizens of Central City.

In this lesson, you had the chance to apply to a planning scenario the knowledge and skills from this course, as well as your job knowledge.

Course Summary

DHS strives to provide its workforce and the nation with tools and training to prevent, protect from, mitigate, respond to, and recover from potential emergencies and disasters. The primary goal of this course is to provide DHS employees—those with and those without a direct planning job function—with basic planning knowledge.

This course provided you with an introduction to and an overview of homeland security planning. We discussed the:

- Purpose and benefits of planning
- Effect of planning on you and homeland security preparedness
- Characteristics and tools of a successful planning effort
- Basic planning process steps
- Mission areas and planning considerations associated with each

In the Planning Learning Activity lesson, you were given a chance to apply your job skills and knowledge, as well as basic planning knowledge from this course to a scenario.

You should now have a better understanding of basic planning and your role in homeland security planning. With this increased knowledge, you are now ready to help DHS achieve its goal of maturing and strengthening the homeland security enterprise.

www.ingramcontent.com/pod-product-compliance
Lightning Source LLC
Chambersburg PA
CBHW081853250726
48659CB00008B/2734